BUSINESS WISE

Disclaimer – This is not for the lazy person, but for THE GO GETTER, the Business-minded. So, what is written below is to encourage seriously minded people who want to excel in their own business.

Have you given thought to owning your own business? Do you realize that you are worth more than your employer pays you? Don't quit your job, but take some time to read this mini book dedicated to your empowerment. No insult meant, but you have allowed others to convince you that you are being paid wages equal to your ability.

I equate being employed to not being in control of your business potential. An 8 – 5 definitely impedes your progression to success and here is why:

You are told what time to arrive and what time to leave

The person(s) at the top of the pyramid make all of the decisions and speak for the masses

You can't make your own hours

You can only work long hours per approval

You can't make major decisions

You can't run the business

You have assigned breaks

You have an assigned lunch periods

You don't have reserved parking

You don't receive bonuses

You are not the CEO

No matter how many good ideas you have, no one listens...

And when they listen, the ideas become theirs

Have you ever been in a meeting and when given the opportunity to speak to what tasks you perform on a daily basis and your manager or other company officer who never has worked in your area thought they knew more than you? Or, if you made a statement that everyone understood (completely), your manager or other company officer felt the need to explain in detail by saying "what _____ meant was...?

Seriously, if you want to become successful and increase your earning potential, you need to take some time, read this book. Devise a plan and work it to fruition and work the plan. There is something about freedom, something about being the decision maker, something about business competition...I WIN!!

Business Wise

For the owner, employee and the Consumer

Customer Service: Service the customer

Customer Care: Care for the customer

Customer Retention: Retain the customer's business

Contents

Know your business area, properties, services needed, upcoming trends, styles and fashions

Visit your competition

Hire an accountant or other tax expert?

What is a sale? A sale is to assist the customer to purchase after you as a salesperson, assist in creating a need for whatever you are selling. When perspective buyers contact or begin an interaction, you ask questions. This is called probing, where you begin to ask open-ended questions (example: what can we help you with today?) By doing so, you gather information and listen and began to lead the customer to be more detailed. Then, you start to lead and make recommendations based on the information gathered. Once an agreement is reached (not the sale), but an understanding that you understand the needs of the customer. Once you've helped to determine the desired product or need, you can close the sale. That is, you have caused the perspective customer to have or create a need, reached an agreement, then subsequently made the sale.

Know your BUSINESS – One's work or occupation; the buying and selling of commodities and services; commerce; trade; store; factory or a commercial or industrial establishment. Will this business be an online one or a standing building? In this book, we will deal specifically with a standing building or buildings, as in various locations. Sounds exciting? It is, one step at a time with smart and hard work!!!

Know your BUDGET – Do you have a budget to cover expenses?

Know your BUSINESS PLAN – Do you know about business planning, a plan for your successful business?

Know how and where to advertise – Do you know enough to advertise your business or will you hire an agency? If the latter, have you budgeted for it?

Know your COMPETITION – Similar business vying or competing for the same customer

Know your CUSTOMERS – One who buys; a consumer

Know your DEMAGRAPHICS – Vital statistics, births, deaths, marriages and populations, broken into segments of areas consisting of racial and ethnic groups and purchasing habits.

Know your P&L – Profit & Loss

Know your business area, PROPERTIES, SERVICES NEEDED, UPCOMING TRENDS, STYLES, and FASHIONS unless you create them.

Visit your competition.

Hire an accountant or other tax expert. You will need to be knowledgeable of state and federal laws regarding sales taxes, exemptions and credits. An expert can also assist with your P&L. If you are knowledgeable enough, you can do this and **save money**. I suggest that you do your research before making this decision.

If you don't know one of these, you are destined for failure. The **Good News** is that you can, and should learn how to be successful. Once you become a business professional or owner, you will have homework and tons of research daily. You want potential customers to know you are open or about to open for business. You open your business every day, but there are no customers. Are you surprised? You did not advertise by making it known to the consumer public that you are opening for business!! So, what is your expectation? You don't expect your business to succeed. There are certain planned and thought out things you that you have to do beforehand in expectation. Even before you write your business plan or purchase the first piece of inventory or office furniture there has to be a vision. No vision/plan equals no success, which equals failure.

You walk into a store or any other place of business and no one notices, no greeting, no acknowledgement. You feel as if no one wants to treat you as a customer, but are willing to accept the benefits ...your cash. If I walk into a place of business, chances are that I'm interested in what is offered or available. Or, at least, browse and maybe, see if there is something I may be interested in buying. When I walk into any place of business, regardless of my appearance, I expect immediate service unless all employees are busy. We are all different, skin color, height, weight, status, dialect and habits. But, once we walk into a place of business, we come under one umbrella...customer. I don't expect to be followed throughout the store because of what I look like or what you think...I am John Q customer. What I do expect is to be acknowledged and asked "may I help you?" Once this happens, I will respond with "I'm just looking", a yes or no. When this is established, you as a salesperson follow my lead. If assistance is needed or if the customer is browsing will dictate your next action. As a customer, we can be pernickety, that is, requiring extremely careful treatment. In other words, we can be precise and/or fussy. In order to give your customer excellent service, you must be able to judge what the attitude is today. Meaning that if there is a next visit, the attitude may be different...so, stay sharp and observant.

As a business owner, I must establish myself as such. But you do not do so in a brutish (gross, savage, stupid, lacking the ability to reason or cruel) manner. You conduct yourself as a **BUSINESS** owner. I capped **BUSINESS** because it is more important to be such than to own such. In other words, you cannot be an owner of such unless it is in existence. And businesses fail daily, not because the product is bad, but because the representation or presentation is bad. How do I present myself as a business owner without being high minded or haughty (showing great pride in oneself, disdain, contempt or scorn for others).

You present yourself as a businessperson or owner. **Remember:** When you were a child, did your parents say to you on a daily basis, "I'm your parent"? Or, did they display certain actions that said to you that they were in control or in authority? They made good decisions and treated you as a child. They took control and directed you in such a manner that your outcome was good. Then, they guided you to a point of making decisions based on their input. But, the great thing about this is you felt that you made the decision on your own. This is what's called good parenting. Take the 'child' out of this scenario and replace it with customer. Now, how well you do this determines how successful you will be.

Customer service means to service the customer. In other words, serve the customer and do so to the best of your professional ability. You have a great understanding of the saying, "the customer is always right". Sorry customers, but you are not always right. Good business persons have the ability to reason with a customer to a point of compromise. It is a win, win situation. Service is something given by a servant. A servant serves the customer. So, who is the servant? Business owner, salesperson, service provider, you are the servant.

Given that you are the servant and the salesperson or business owner, you determine your success. This is a unique situation because there are no limitations, whether you take advantage of it or not.

How well you treat your customers, including perspective ones, will determine most of your success. When a person walks into your place of business, they become a customer regardless of whether there is a purchase or not. When someone calls or visits your place of business they are to be treated like an old friend, a beloved relative or like that movie star that you love so dearly. When we interact, I feel royal, rich, beautiful, handsome, special and welcomed. Good customer service dictates that I feel welcomed and upon my departure I should feel that you look forward to seeing me again. Once again, even if I don't buy anything you make me feel this way. From my first greeting to my departure there is a feeling that I'll be back. You as an owner or employee must have a genuine love for people...you are a people person.

Real estate, insurance, clothing/fashion, fast food, lending, restaurant, convenience store, auto sales, grocery store and any other sales or service outlets can become a more successful business. **Caution: Owning a business means long hours, hard work, being knowledgeable, a positive attitude and a friendly smile.** So, if you want to leave your **8 to 5** because of hard work and long hours, I suggest that you apply for a job elsewhere and not pursue business ownership.

As a business owner, you have to insure that all associates, employees, investors and vendors share your vision and attitude towards business and customers. Not that you want to have clones, but someone who shares your vision. Your business and all entities reflect your attributes and character as a businessperson and individual. Wherever you go, how you treat people, how you react to various stimuli and your overall demeanor says very specifically to your customers who they are doing business with.

Customer service, as we stated, is providing the **BEST** service to your customers at **ALL** times in **ALL** situations. When persons show the slightest interest in your business, they become potential customers and by business standards, deserve the highest level of treatment. Remember, tangibles are normally sold face to face or via the telephone or online. And intangibles are sold via telephone or online. Tangibles are things you can eat, see, feel/touch/wear, and smell or hear and intangibles are mostly services where you can only see the benefits, such as long distance services, insurance or utilities.

Mr. or Ms. Customer calls you. They are not strangers, but a familiar voice who is calling to ask for advice, input, information, or pricing, which you're hoping will lead to a visit to your place of business. If possible, please do not place your customers on hold for more than one minute. People tend to get agitated after being placed on hold. If the hold time will be more than a minute, have someone else handle the call or give the customer the option of being called back by you. Confirm the telephone number and be very specific about the callback time. After the initial self- intro you need to get the customer's name. Make sure you address the customer as they desire, Mr., Ms., Mrs. or first name, if preferred. You need to be **a people person**. The customer needs to feel as if they have known you forever. Some business people are naturals and some have to learn. No matter how busy you are, take a deep breath and prepare for a conversation full of questions regarding inventory, sizes, pricing, services, comparisons and "how long have you been in business...and the greatest question of all "where are you located?" Now, you are ready to do business!!! Once your customer's questions have been answered, you start to probe: Where or how did you get our number? Are you familiar with the area where we are located? When can we expect to see you? Based on the customer's interests, you start to offer services and/or merchandise based on the customer's interests or requests. At this point you should have developed a rapport and the trust barrier has been taken down and your customer has allowed you to take charge based on your expertise and exhibited leadership ability.

When customers visit your business, welcome them with open arms and a big smile. Remember, your success depends on your ability to present yourself as an integral part of your business...one customer at a time. First impressions will determine whether you will have repeat customers and repeat business. And, repeat customers help to build what's called a customer base or generally referred to as clientele. You can't have bad days in business that are obvious to your customers. When perspective customers visit your establishment, their initial experience will determine a lasting impression. No matter what goods your business offer, how the customer is treated will be an everlasting memory. When customers are treated with dignity they tend to tell others about their experience. When they are treated great or poorly, they tell their acquaintances. Don't shoot yourself in the foot, make wise decisions.

Before starting your sales pitch, show the customer around the place of business. Give them your business card and a brief history. Talk about the neighborhood, other businesses in the community and other owners and safety. Be very careful not to say anything negative about other businesses, specifically, your competition. Then, slowly start the sales interview: What can we help you with? You don't use the word "I" but "we". We denotes a cohesive group of people with the same philosophy, attitude, sincerity, professionalism, concerns, honesty, integrity and friendliness. Depending on the mood of the customer, allow them to browse briefly then say "let me know if you have any questions." Always smile and be engaged and show an eagerness to assist. Please don't follow the customer around the store, but allow them to browse. Usually, if a customer is interested in purchasing something that decision was made prior to walking into your place of business. In other words, if they see something they want, they will purchase it. Once you see an interest, casually walk over and ask "do you have any questions about this" or just start offering information about the product. If there is no resistance, continue offering assistance in a non-aggressive manner. Offer information regarding the price and any other information regarding the item(s).

If a door for conversation opens, tell the customer how important they are to your business and why you chose the area. Let them know that you are excited to have the opportunity to serve the community and willingness to receive input from your customers. Make sure you have a list to be used to document name, phone number and email address of all of your customers. We will discuss this in more detail when we cover **customer care** and **customer retention**. If you are the only person in the business, you may have to limit your conversation if another customer comes in. But, being a seasoned salesperson, you should be able to hold multiple conversations with two or more customers regarding the same topic, but addressing various questions. If your customer base dictates, you should hire additional part-time or fulltime salespersons if needed. That way, your customers never suffer or feel abandoned if you become overwhelmed. Having an abundance of customers is a blessing, but you have to plan to accommodate them and meet their small or demanding needs. Whether your customers spend $2.00 or $2000.00 dollars, the value of each is the same. In other words, one customer may spend $2000.00 dollars today, but will not return for three months, whereas the $2.00 customer may shop two times per week, spending various amounts which equals $2000.00 or more during the next three months. No customer can spend too little and never too much. Don't be so excited about a $2000.00 customer that you don't value the ones that spend the minimal.

You take care of all of your customers, nurturing each one to the point of becoming faithful ones that help build your base. You are not a business without customers. As customers, they expect you to offer a service or goods at a fair and competitive price. There is one exception...as a customer, I have knowingly paid higher prices because of the service rendered to me. Sometimes it is worth the cost to pay more when treated special. There is this one convenience store I frequent. It won my patronage on my initial visit. When I walked in, they... all of the employees greeted me with "welcome to __!! Upon my departure, the cashier stated "we'll see you tomorrow". They sell fresh coffee and hot chocolate as well as donuts. Because of this I bypass other similar businesses to patronize this particular one, even if their gas prices are sometimes higher. As customers, we become attached and bond to businesses that provide excellent customer service. This is human nature, that is, we are drawn to this particular type of stimuli. There is a barber shop in our neighborhood where the owner insist that his employees greet each customer with a verbal acknowledgement, smile and handshake. This became common practice for customers, not only did we expect it, we started doing the same thing. There is also a certain dress code and expected behavior from the employee as well as the customers. I enjoy this place so much that I don't take advantage of the senior discount because of my age, but choose to pay the going rate. As customers, our behavior is reciprocal. That is, we respond to treatment received...when shown love or respect, we show the same. This is not rocket science, you simply reap what you sow.

Good customer service is the basis for excellent customer care. The first or initial contact with prospective customers will determine whether they will return. Customer care is how your customer will be cared for. As stated previously, before your customer leaves your business, make sure you have phone number(s), email addresses and mailing address. Also, ask for referrals. If the customers did not make a purchase keep in contact with them. After the initial visit, make contact the next day or sooner to let them know that you appreciate their patronage. If via email or us mail you may send an appropriate, but short questionnaire to get a basic overview of their initial experience. Ask short, but open-ended questions like "what did you like most or least about our business?" "When can we expect another visit?" Finally, ask "how do you rate our customer service". Warning, the response you receive will be helpful, but sometimes very painful, but they all will be extremely helpful. If the customer made a purchase insert a printed thank you note in the package and immediately send a thank you email with the same questionnaire format. Once monthly, send email or mail your customer regarding upcoming sales, new products or services followed by a phone call. And, retention will depend on your diligence. Organize your contact files, you will need every prospective customer to help build your business. You have to be patient, smart, persistent and consistent in building your business. This is not an overnight process. Work the plan and plan the work. Work smarter and harder towards attaining your goal and excellent customer care is a great start.

Customer Retention means that you retain your customers' business, therefore maintaining your customer base. Excellent customer service plus excellent customer care equals customer retention. Based on how well you performed at service and care determines the success of customer retention. And, the success of retention determines the longevity of your thriving business. You need to plan quarterly events for your customers with the focus being on them. Make them the focus of the business oriented celebration. Sponsor non-alcoholic and drug and tobacco free events that will have previews of upcoming business. If retail, a preview of newly received fashion items. If real estate, then updates of recent properties on the market. Whatever your business ownership, make the celebration customer oriented. Have your customers RSVP with their acceptance and the number in their parties. Yes, encourage them to bring guests with the understanding that this is business oriented and make sure everyone understands the rules, specifically no alcohol nor drugs. You want your customers to feel safe and you are maintaining a positive business image.

NOTE: It is your responsibility to insure that your customers are safe at all times while patronizing your business. Have an established relationship with law enforcement in the event there is loitering or pan handling. These activities tend to frighten customers and creates a negative business image.

Know your business, know your business, and know your business!! An owner is responsible for knowing the business and be able to answer and elaborate on it. You do so by studying, research and constantly reading. In other words, due diligence is a must. Talk to other business owners that are not in the same profession. You do this to learn about overall business philosophies and practices. When we say "know your business" it means to have an understanding of various concepts and comparatively see the relationship to yours. You may find that some beliefs and practices can be improved by modifications or that they are simply out dated. Be sure that you understand various terminologies and be able to explain them.

Know your Mission Statement. You define your business' ethics, goals, norms, culture for decision-making. What your business does for its employees and what it does for its owners (if there are partners or investors).

Know your budget. This is where the proverbial rubber meets the road. Do you have the finances to cover your business expenses without borrowing from family, business associates or lending institutions? This is why you need to know your business plan because it is dependent on your budget. Don't over plan, but perform simple mathematics. Each business component has an associated cost. If your plan cost exceeds your budget, don't close shop, but revise your plan. Do not seek financing unless absolutely necessary.

Revision of your initial plan to fit your existing budget should be your first step. Probably, the most expensive startup cost is the building used to house the business, then the cost of advertisements, décor, inventory, licenses and utilities. Start small with what you can afford based on your budget, then grow your size as your net revenue grows. If you are attempting to purchase the building, try working out a rent to own agreement with the owner. If this is not feasible, you may have to start online if possible, but make this a last resort decision.

Most philosophies state that you are successful if you can meet your expenses after the first year of business and that most new businesses fail during the first year. If you believe this, you are doomed for failure!! The missing part of this equation is your desire and ability to succeed. Most businesses fail due to the **lack of proper planning.** Having faith requires that you do what is necessary to succeed in your endeavor. Faith is an action word…in other words, you will show your faith by your works. And, faith without works is dead being left alone. Finance or the lack thereof is not the issue here, planning, action and work can be the big problem. **Plan the work and work the plan!!**

Know your Business Plan. Your business plan is a concise thought out plan of approach based on data and information results from: Your business, your budget, how you plan to advertise, your competition, your customers, demographics, your P&L, business areas, properties, services needed, trends, styles and fashions.

Know how and where to advertise. Do not hire an agency to advertise your goods and services. New businesses, particularly small ones do not need an agency, simply because you cannot afford it. Also, they lack the personal touch and the emotional investment. Two things that will help more than anything else: 1. **<u>Free</u>** Social media. There are several outlets that can be utilized to advertise your goods and services. You have the flexibility of investing personally, as much time as possible and your emotions. You can reach the world without leaving your home or business. 2. **Word of mouth via customers.** As a business owner, you drive this by how well you treat your customers. Go back and read **<u>customer service, customer care and customer retention.</u>** 3. Dress your windows and exterior in an attractive business manner to attract prospective customers. When you dress your windows or exterior, it is intended to draw from the traffic flow by exciting the curiosity of prospective customers. Initially, things may be slow, but with consistent and powerful advertisements you will began to see gradual to modest improvements in the form of customer base and revenue. Although, some days will be slow and others great, don't base your success on either, but chart the individual days to determine what drove the more successful ones. Then, look at the average of your number of business days per week to determine not only the gross amount, but the average gross amount. Then start to look at monthly and quarterly amounts so you can chart your increases and decreases and look at the advertisements at that time.

Know your competition. You simply do this by reading, studying, and calling and visiting similar various stores and businesses, talking to customers, ask questions and basic spying.

Know your customers. You get to know your customers by interaction, observation and documentation. A Dossier of each customer containing their likes and dislikes of the goods or services offered by your business. Learn and remember their idiosyncrasies because by doing so, you will be able to know likes, dislikes and partialities. As we stated before, some customers are pernickety and will need special attention. Some customers are moody and irritable, but these people drive your business successes. Get to know their shopping habits, what type items they purchase and the amounts spent. You may also note the intervals of purchases and the amounts spent. How well do you know your customers' family members? Spouse and children's names? Customers' birthdates so you can always send a greeting or gift? You are investing time in your customers and they are investing money in your business. When customers feel that you are interested in them, they become more interested in your business and will be more willing to support it.

Know your demographics. As stated previously, demographics is vital statistics, births, deaths, marriages and populations, broken into segments of areas consisting of racial and ethnic groups and purchasing habits. You want to pay special attention to this area, its purchasing habits based on racial and ethnic groups.

Most people think that race and ethnic group means the same thing. **Ethnic** means nations or groups neither Christian nor Jewish; heathen. Designating or of any of the basic divisions or groups of mankind, as distinguished by customs, characteristics and language. **Race** is simply Black (African American); White (Caucasian) or Yellow (Mongoloid). Now, within these races, there may be what is called ethnicity: the fact or state of belonging to a social group that has a common national or cultural tradition. An ethnic group is a group that has a distinct culture of its own and tends to share an ancestral heritage. Race tends to be a group identified by physical characteristics. An African American and a Black Dominican are the same race, but not of the same ethnicity.

Then, you need to have an understanding of this and where these people live within your target areas. Know their shopping habits, but not necessarily by race or ethnicity. Since this is somewhat tricky and sticky, I suggest doing a random sampling. Nothing long and drawn out, just a simple sampling to determine shopping habits and type of goods and services purchased and distance driven to purchase such. **Hence, hard**

to get desired goods and services made easy equals increased revenue possibilities!!!

Know Your P & L. If this is your first business, you need to just grasp an understanding. So, let's go... P & L means profit and loss. The gain or loss from business transactions applied, especially to a bookkeeping account at the close of a **fiscal** year (the twelve-month period between settlements of financial accounts). A year reckoned for taxing or accounting purposes. 365 (6) days that does not necessarily correspond to the calendar year beginning January 1st. When doing this, it may be important to remember two words/terms: 1. Cost prohibitive – describes something that is difficult to obtain because of its cost. 2. Exponentially - Something's increasing quickly by large amounts. Great degrees or great amounts.

Know your business area, properties, services needed, upcoming trends, styles and fashions. This happens when you know your demographics, competition and customers.

Visit your competition. You have to do this if plans are to be successful. Not only are you looking at their inventory, but how they treat customers and associates. You are also looking for competitive pricing and services as well as traffic flow.

Hire an accountant or other tax expert? If you don't have tax experience, you will need help from a professional at least for the first year. Shop for this professional like you do for other services and goods. Insure that this person and/or business is reputable, being honest and professional. You will need to decide if you will have only a business license and an incorporation or the former only. The incorporation provides a seal and protection of your business name. In other words, no one can legally use your business name. There are some mandatory things you have to do in order to be compliant, locally, statewide and federal. There are decisions to be made regarding sales tax payments in intervals of monthly or quarterly and the benefits of doing so.

Depending on the locality or city, there are costs for business licenses as well as any signage on your standing structure. Also, there are various inspections by the city and fire department. If there are modifications required, you need guidance and directives.

There are so many tax deductions, but you have to know which are applicable to your type of business. For example, do you use a portion of your dwelling place for storage or a second office? If so, you can claim a portion of your square footage (an equation) as a deduction. There is no end to owning a profitable business if you are faithful in your endeavor.

Training your Associates. My first piece of advice is **"Never rely on memory when training someone".** The **first** thing to do is to create a training manual with the mission statement on the first page. The **second** thing is to give each associate a copy of the manual. Make sure that each associate reads this manual prior to training. Each associate needs to understand your business mission statement and speak the same language without deviation. When each associate says the same thing about everything, there is no room for confusion, particularly for or with the customer. A well run business is a well-trained business staff. Training is not an option, but a very mandatory action for everyone including the business owner. After training, there should be testing to insure that everyone was able to grasp the information. Once training is complete, the manual becomes a reference manual for trained associates. Do addendums (additions or supplements) when there are changes to your business.

If possible do your training online or make plans to transition from your manual one when possible or affordable.

Preparation for opening. Now that you have accomplished all other goals, you are at the stage where you prepare for opening your business.

You will need to solicit assistance from the following businesses/services/agencies:

Local government

Police

US Post Office

Social Media

Radio stations

Grocery stores

Catering services

You will contact the local government or municipality for notification of the event and obtain permits if required. Then, notify your local police department that additional presence will be requested for your event. Usually, both agencies are very cooperative when new businesses are opening in there city.

You will need to visit your **local post office** and get all zip codes within thirty miles of your area. Then, you will do a mass mailing to these one month prior to opening. Follow-up with announcements via social media and radio.

Next, you need to contact a caterer. Hopefully you know someone that is inexpensive. You need the type of food that will feed one hundred or two hundred if served as finger food. Go shopping at your local grocery store or market for items like fruit, dips and non-alcoholic beverages.

Initial/Grand Opening. Okay, you have completed your due diligence and ready for your initial/grand opening. Samplings of your goods or services offered. You and your staff are in place to pass out business cards, serve and present your goods. As difficult as it may seem, you and your staff will interact with each guest, getting as much information as possible. The intent is to insure each guest that you are sincere about providing quality services and becoming an integral part of their community.

That's it, I think we are on the road to another successful business venture.

God bless you!!!